Wiggle
TAMERS

BY JOLENE L. ROEHLKEPARTAIN

Group

Loveland, Colorado

DEDICATION

To my sister, Nancy,
who delights in every child she meets—
and they delight in her.

WIGGLE TAMERS

Copyright © 1995 Jolene L. Roehlkepartain

CREDITS
Book Acquisitions Editor: Mike Nappa
Editors: Stephen Parolini and Jan Kershner
Senior Editor: Beth Rowland Wolf
Creative Products Director: Joani Schultz
Copy Editor: Ann Marie Rozum
Art Director and Designer: Jean Bruns
Cover Art Director: Liz Howe
Cover Designer: Rich Martin
Computer Graphic Artist: Joyce Douglas
Cover Photographer: Craig DeMartino
Illustrator: Kate Flanagan
Production Manager: Gingar Kunkel

Unless otherwise noted, Scriptures quoted from The Youth Bible, New Century Version, Copyright © 1991 by Word Publishing, Dallas, Texas 75039. Used by permission.

Library of Congress Cataloging-in-Publication Data
Roehlkepartain, Jolene L., 1962-
    Wiggle tamers / by Jolene L. Roehlkepartain.
      p.   cm.
    ISBN 1-55945-615-9
    1. Amusements. 2. Games. I. Title.
    GV1203.R5828   1995
    790.19'922--dc20   95-21946
                                           CIP

10 9 8 7 6 5 4 3 2   04 03 02 01 00 99 98 97 96
Printed in the United States of America.

CONTENTS

Section 3: WIGGLE TAMERS FOR GRADES 4–6

Section 4: WIGGLE TAMERS FOR MIXED AGES

When Wiggles and Giggles Rule

"My mom needs flowers!" Michael shouted as the children ran outside for a break from the lesson. Soon the entire group was giggling and talking as they picked dandelions and wildflowers.

I listened to their conversations and wondered: How much of the lesson will these children remember when a butterfly can distract them mid-sentence?

I thought about why we had taken a break. Lauren had started singing while Michael was pestering the assistant teacher for a story about dinosaurs. Lee had wandered to another part of the room and discovered a car hidden behind some blocks. The others were looking at the ceiling, or whispering knock-knock jokes and giggling with the answers. Only a couple of children were really engaged in the lesson.

After working with children for 16 years, I've learned the importance of breaks. Sometimes all children need is a quick, structured activity that can shake out their wiggles and tame their giggles. That's what *Wiggle Tamers* is: a book with 101 age-appropriate, sure-fire, easy-to-use activities to get the wiggles out.

To make the most of a Wiggle Tamer activity, it pays to be prepared. Choose four or five activities before your lesson and bring any needed supplies to class. Or create a Wiggle Tamer Shelf in your classroom (see the box on next page) so you'll be ready for fun on the spur of the moment. Read through the

Wiggle Tamer activities ahead of time so you'll be familiar with them when the time comes to "tame a wiggle" in class. During your lesson, when you notice the children starting to squirm and lose their concentration, put the lesson on "pause" and jump in with one of these activities. It's nearly impossible to *plan* a certain time to do these activities, but as you watch your children, you'll know exactly when you need one.

The Wiggle Tamer Shelf

Wiggle Tamers work especially well when they can happen on the spur of the moment. To help "create" spontaneity, you may want to create a Wiggle Tamer Shelf of easy-to-find supplies in your classroom. Then, when it's time for a Wiggle Tamer—just raid the shelf! Here are some common, everyday items you might want to include on your shelf:

- Balls (all shapes and sizes)
- Blindfolds (bandannas or scarves)
- Bubble bath
- Buckets or tubs
- Chalk
- Coffee cans
- Colored balloons
- Construction paper
- Cotton balls
- Crayons and pencils
- Empty boxes
- Envelopes
- Facial tissues
- Jelly beans
- Magnifying glasses
- Newsprint
- Newspapers
- Old sheets
- Paper cups and plates
- Scissors
- Squirt bottles
- Straws
- Tape
- Toilet paper
- Yarn

Here are some tips to help you get the most out of a Wiggle Tamer activity:

● **Choose activities that match your lesson.** If your kids are learning about Noah, try water activities such as "Squirt Away!" activity 71, or "Squirt Tag," activity 86. If you're studying about Joseph, do "Joseph's Coat," activity 29. Plus, you can adapt activities as necessary to match other lesson topics.

● **Plan to use messy or wet activities only when you know kids will be casually dressed,** such as at midweek meetings, during after-school programs, or on retreats.

● **Ask for donations.** Some activities in this book require a few materials—the kinds of things most households have on hand. Create a list of needed items and give it to parents. If they can't fill your shelves, ask the rest of the congregation for donations.

● **Be excited.** Introduce each activity with enthusiasm and children will respond in kind.

● **Include everybody.** Many of these activities encourage children to interact with each other. Help children to be involved.

● **Demonstrate the activity.** Show children how the activity works while you explain how to do it. Children understand new concepts better when they see *and* hear how they work.

● **Don't dally.** Remember, the main objective is to return to the lesson. Jump back into your lesson as soon as the Wiggle Tamer ends.

● **Add your own ideas.** Once you use these activities, you'll quickly see other ways to help children release energy in creative, fun ways. Don't overlook another important resource: your creative children. And if you want additional ideas, get a copy of Group's *Fidget Busters*—a book which has another 101 wiggle tamers for children.

● **Have fun!**

And remember: The next time children start wiggling, roaming, wandering, whispering, and dallying, don't groan. The fun is about to begin! Just announce a new activity that gets children jumping and giggling. Before you know it, you'll have recaptured that fleeting attention span and will be on your way with the rest of your lesson.

SECTION 1

Wiggle Tamers

for Preschoolers

Hug God's Earth

Take the children outside. Point out items from nature that are in your church's yard or parking lot, such as trees, leaves, and grass.

Say: **We're going to play Hug God's Earth. When I tell you to hug something, run over and put your arms around it. Ready? Let's play!**

Call out commands such as—

- Hug a leaf
- Hug a tree
- Hug a friend
- Hug the church
- Hug a teacher
- Hug a stick
- Hug the grass (or snow)

Then say: **Let's give ourselves one big hug before we get back to our lesson.** Form a group hug before heading back to class.

Balloon Grab

(You'll need 17 balloons: four yellow, four green, four blue, one orange, and four red.)

Inflate the balloons. Place all the balloons—except for the orange one—in the middle of the room or field. Keep the orange balloon near your lesson book.

Say: **I'm going to name a color. If you see a balloon that color on the ground, grab it and run all around with it. If you can't grab one, follow someone who has that color balloon.**

Then when I name another color, everyone is to drop their balloons and grab the color balloon I named. Again, if you can't grab one, follow someone who has that color balloon.

Start by naming yellow. Then after a minute or so name a different color. Repeat the activity five or six times. End by naming all the colors.

Then say: **Orange!** Grab the orange balloon and hold it high.

Say: **Now follow me as we go back to our lesson!**

Nursery Rhyme Ruckus

Have children stand in a large circle.

Say: **We're going to play Nursery Rhyme Ruckus. One person will sing the first word of a nursery rhyme while doing an action. Then the person on his or her right must sing the second word of the song and do a new action. The third person must then sing the third word of the song and do yet another action. We'll take turns around the circle until we've finished one verse of the song. Choose actions that match your word, if possible.**

Here's an example of how this works: **Row** *(child pretends to row)*, **row** *(child pretends to row)*, **row** *(child pretends to row)*, **your** *(child points to someone else)*, **boat** *(child pretends to sit in a boat, bobbing up and down)*, and so on.

When you finish a verse of a nursery rhyme, have the next person in the circle choose another rhyme to begin. Do three or four rhymes.

Then say: **Now let's play Ring Around the Rosy and then all fall down in our seats.**

4

Sudsy Stamp

(You'll need three or four tubs filled with water and bubble bath.)

Right before you do this activity, have an adult fill three or four tubs with water and bubble bath. Use a brand that really makes the suds! Have kids form pairs, and have partners hold hands.

Say: **We'll move these soap bubbles to the floor. When I say "go," we'll go stamp out the sudsy bubbles to make them disappear. We want to be careful, though, because suds can be slippery! So be sure to hold your partner's hand to help your partner keep from falling while you're stamping. If someone does fall, move away from him or her until that person can get up.**

When kids are ready and the bubbles have formed, have an adult scoop out the bubbles and shake them onto the floor. Say: **Ready? Go!**

Allow a few moments for kids to stamp. Keep an eye out for any kids who might slip. When all the bubbles have been stamped, say: **Now let's stamp on imaginary soap bubbles as we head back to our lesson.**

(*Variation:* If you'd rather not have kids stamping on bubbles, you might want to blow bubbles using a bubble wand and have children chase the bubbles.)

Time for Church

Say: **Let's pretend we're in a church that does every-thing in fast-motion. Do what I do as our imaginary worship service begins.** Perform the following actions with the children, moving as quickly as you can from one motion to the next.

- Sit in a pew.
- Stand to pray.
- Sit in a pew.
- Sing a hymn. (Sing "Jesus Loves Me.")
- Take an offering. (Pass a basket.)
- Stand and say "hi" to each other.
- Sit in a pew.
- Listen to the minister. (Cup one hand around an ear.)
- Sing another hymn. (Sing one of your group's favorites.)
- Stand to pray.
- Hold hands and say "amen."

Then say: **Let's all shake hands and thank everyone for coming to the worship service before we walk back to our lesson.**

God's Kingdom

Say: **Let's pretend we're Adam and Eve taking care of God's world. Do what I do to take care of God's wonderful animals and plants.** (Pretend to do the following activities as you describe them.)

- **Let's water the plants.**
- **Let's feed the animals.**
- **Let's plant some seeds.**
- **Let's breathe the clean air.**
- **Let's wash a dirty skunk.**
- **Let's put a baby kangaroo back in its mother's pouch.**

Then say: **Let's each carry a soft baby tiger and put it quietly to bed before we get back to our lesson.**

Colors Together

Have the children look at the colors they are wearing. Take note of the colors that more than one child is wearing.

Say: **When I name a color, anyone wearing that color can bow while the rest of us applaud. For example, if I call out "blue!" and Jeremy and Tony are wearing blue, then Jeremy and Tony can bow while the rest of us applaud for them.**

When kids understand the rules, call out the first color. Repeat the activity several times, making sure that everyone has a chance to bow and be applauded.

Then say: **Let's all applaud for each other. Then as a big, colorful group, let's all bow as we go back to our lesson.**

Circles, Squares, and Triangles

(You'll need three pieces of newsprint, masking tape, and crayons.)

Tape three pieces of newsprint on different walls of the room. Draw a huge circle on one, a huge square on another, and a huge triangle on the third.

Say: **We're going to play a shape game. When I call out a shape, I want you to find the newsprint with that shape and run to it. Then draw that same shape on that paper.**

Give each child a crayon. Say:

● **Boys, find the square; Girls, find the triangle.**
(Pause for children to draw. Give children lots of time after you call out a shape, and applaud their efforts even if they don't draw well.)

● **Girls, find the circle; Boys, find the triangle.**
(Pause for children to draw.)

● **Boys, find the circle; Girls, find the square.** (Pause for children to draw.)

● **Girls *and* Boys, find your favorite shape and draw it again on the paper!** (Pause for children to draw.)

Finish by saying: **Now that we're in great *shape*, let's find the rest of our lesson!**

Bedtime Routine

Say: **We're going to pretend it's bedtime. I want you to name something you do before going to bed, then we'll all pretend we're doing that with you. Let's think of as many things as we can.**

If children have trouble, you might mention some of these bedtime activities:

- Brushing teeth
- Having a snack
- Reading a story
- Getting a back rub
- Saying a prayer
- Putting on pajamas
- Snuggling under the covers
- Turning out the lights
- Saying, "Good night"

Have the children do five or six actions. Then say: **Now it's time to wake up and go back to our lesson.**

(*Note:* If your children particularly enjoy this activity, you might also want to try the activity called "Good Morning" with your kids. That activity is found in the book *Fidget Busters,* available from Group Publishing, Inc.)

Compass Kids

Have children stand and stretch.

Say: **We're going to play Compass Kids. When I name something, I want you to point to it as quickly as you can.**

Name items such as—

- A door
- A Bible
- A chair
- A window
- A boy
- A desk
- A girl
- A teacher

Then say: **Now let's see if we can find our lesson.**

Broken Dishes

(You'll need a paper plate for each child.)

Give each child a paper plate, then have the children skip around the room while holding onto their plates. Whenever you say, "Broken dishes," have the children drop their plates and shout "uh-oh!"

Then have children pretend to clean up the mess. After they pick up their plates, let them continue to skip until you call out "Broken dishes" again.

Repeat the activity three or four times.

Then say: **Let's set the table back at our lesson to find out what's cooking.** Have children take their plates back to your lesson area to place neatly on the floor or table before you continue with the lesson.

Big Jump!

Have children stand up. Say: **We're going to play Big Jump. When I say somebody's name, I want everyone to shout that person's name and jump high into the air. Ready?**

Repeat the activity a number of times so everyone gets a chance to have his or her name called. If you have a large class, you may want to call two or three names at the same time during the activity. Then hold up the Bible or your lesson book.

Call out "Bible" and have kids respond. Say: **Now that we've jumped and shouted for the Bible, let's find out more about what's inside.**

Red Sea Chase

(Review Exodus 14:5-31 for a background on the Bible story that inspires this activity.)

Have children "travel" around the room as if they are Moses and the Israelites leaving Egypt.

Say: **Let's pretend we're Moses' friends. We want to get away from Pharaoh and the bad guys. When I say, "Watch out for the bad guys," get down on the floor and crawl as fast as you can around the room! When I say, "The bad guys are stuck in the Red Sea," stop where you are and rest.**

When everyone is ready, start the activity by saying: **Watch out for bad guys!**

Do the activity a number of times. Then say: **While the bad guys are stuck in the Red Sea, let's hurry back to our lesson.**

Crowded Island

(You'll need masking tape or chalk.)

Use masking tape to outline an "island" (a circle with an approximate eight-foot radius) on the floor or use chalk to draw a circle on the pavement outside.

Say: **We're going to play Crowded Island. I want everyone to crowd inside this circle without anyone stepping outside the line.**

While everyone is gathering in the circle, outline a smaller circle within stepping distance of the first. Say: **Uh-oh! The tide is coming in and covering up this island! We'll have to move to a new island!** Encourage kids to move to the second island while you outline yet another, even smaller island.

Continue having kids move to smaller islands until they're on the smallest island that can hold them. Then say: **Oh! The tide is going out again and uncovering our islands. Let's hop back the way we came.** Have kids go "island-hopping" back to the original circle.

Then say: **Whew! We sure had to squish together on those islands. Now let's go back to our lesson where we can really spread out.**

Silly Stretches

Say: **Did you know your body can stretch and do funny things? Follow me as we make our bodies stretch in different ways.**

Have the children follow you as you give and act out the instructions.

- **We can be wide.**
- **We can be thin.**
- **We can be tall.**
- **We can be short.**
- **We can stretch out our arms.**
- **We can hug ourselves.**
- **We can put our feet far apart.**
- **We can put our feet on top of each other.**
- **We can stretch out and hold hands.**

Wrap up by saying: **Now let's "stretch" our minds by going back to our lesson.**

Upside-Down Greetings

Have children walk around the room. Whenever you say, "Upside-down hi," have children pair up standing back to back, bend over, peer through their legs at their partners, and say "hi!" to each other. You may want to demonstrate this for children before beginning.

Caution kids to be careful not to bump heads on anything or anyone standing near them. Then begin the fun!

Repeat the activity many times so children can pair up with lots of different partners. Soon everybody will be giggling.

Finish by saying: **Let's do an upside-down hi to our lesson!**

Balloon Shake

(You'll need about 10 balloons and an old sheet.)
Inflate the balloons before the activity.

Say: **We're going to play Balloon Shake. Everyone grab a side of this old sheet and pull tightly so that it doesn't touch the ground. Then I'll place balloons on the sheet, one at a time. We'll all flap the sheet to make the balloons bounce, but we'll try not to let any of the balloons fall off. Ready? Let's go!**

Start with one balloon. Gradually add balloons until all are on the sheet.

After the activity, say: **Now let's all bounce ourselves back to our lesson.** Have kids pretend to be balloons as they bounce back to their seats.

Busy Beaver

Say: **Let's pretend we're busy beavers. We'll start by lying on the floor and sleeping as if it's night.** Have everyone lie on the floor. Then act out the following actions with the children as you say them.

- **The beaver wakes up.**
- **The beaver eats a big breakfast.**
- **The beaver says, "Good morning," to another beaver.**
- **The beaver chews on some trees.**
- **The beaver carries a stick in its mouth.**
- **The beaver eats lunch.**
- **The beaver takes a nap.**
- **The beaver marches to pick up sticks.**
- **The beaver builds a beaver house.**
- **The beaver hears a dog and runs in circles.**
- **The beaver hides in the beaver house.**
- **The beaver has dinner.**
- **The beaver reads books with the family.**
- **The beaver goes to bed.**

Finish by saying: **Then the beaver remembers that he never got to hear the end of today's lesson! So the beaver quietly gets up and goes back to his seat to learn something new.**

Run and Touch

Have children line up against one wall of a large recreation room, or against the building if you're outside.

Say: **We're going to play Run and Touch. When I name an object, I want you to run toward it, touch it, then run back to where you started next to the wall.**

Start the activity by naming things in your area. It's usually best to name a larger object that several kids can touch at once, such as a table or a tree, rather than a smaller one such as a button or a light switch.

If you're indoors, consider calling out objects such as a wall, a table, a sink, or a teacher. If you're outside, consider calling out objects such as a fence, a tree, a nearby building, a sidewalk, or playground equipment. Make sure to caution children about traffic or other hazards.

After several "run and touch" rounds, say: **Now let's run back to our lesson.** Have children run back and sit down for the continuation of the lesson.

Color Prayer

(You'll need construction paper of various colors—
enough for each child to have one sheet.)

Give children each one sheet of colored construction
paper and tell them that you're going to say a color prayer.
Explain that you'll name a color during the prayer, and the
person with that color paper will hold it high above his or
her head until another color is mentioned.

Practice this once with your class. Name one color at a
time so children can practice identifying the color and
holding their papers up.

Once children get the hang of the activity, say a prayer
similar to this, pausing after each color to allow kids time
to hold up their papers: **Thank you, God, for colors. We
love the yellow sun that shines in the blue sky. We
love the red roses that bloom near the green grass.
We love to eat red apples and purple grapes. Thank
you, God, for red crayons and orange markers. Thank
you for purple cars and yellow Big Birds. Thank you,
God, for green dinosaurs and red wagons. Thank you,
God, for all the colors. Amen.**

Be sure to include all the colors represented by the children's papers as you pray. Then say: **Let's find the colors
in our lesson book,** and return to the lesson.

Birds and Bees

Say: **We're going to play Birds and Bees. When I say "bird," flap your arms and pretend to fly around the room. When I say "bee," buzz around the room making the sounds of a bee.**

Give the children a moment to practice being birds and bees, then call out "bird" to start the activity. Throughout the game, alternate saying "bird" and "bee." Play several rounds.

To end the activity, say: **Let's be like busy bees and buzz back to our lesson.**

(*Variation:* For extra fun, have some children be birds at the same time other children are being bees. For example, you might have all the boys be birds and all the girls be bees. Or you could have children wearing yellow be bees, while everyone else is a bird.)

God's House

(Use this fun activity to initiate cleanup time.)

Say: **When we take care of God's house, God is pleased. Since the room is kind of messy, let's all hop on one foot and pick up one thing to put away.**

Have children each pick up one item. If there are still more items lying around, have children repeat the activity. Continue until the room is clean.

Then say: **Now let's hop back to our lesson so we can learn other ways to please God.**

23

Clapping Time

Take time for some clapping fun. Start by saying: **It's clapping time! Everybody start clapping!**

Have children clap for a minute or so. Then say: **Now it's smiling time! Everybody show your best smiles!**

Every minute or so, change the action by calling out: **Now it's** (blank) **time!** Fill in the blank with ideas such as—

- Hopping
- Singing (sing a short song such as "Jesus Loves the Little Children")
- Laughing
- Rub-your-belly
- Pat-your-head
- Sit-in-a-circle

Continue as long as you like, but be sure to end with "sit-in-a-circle time." Then say: **Now that we're all in a circle, let's have some back-to-our-lesson time.**

24

Encouragement Practice

Have children gallop like horses around the room. As they gallop, call out an action involving sharing or caring, then have the children do that action. Use the following ideas or come up with your own.

- Shake someone's hand and say, "I'm glad you're here!"
- Smile at a friend.
- Rub a friend's shoulders.
- Say to someone, "I think you're neat!"
- Give a friend a high five.
- Hold someone's hand.

Then say: **While you're still holding hands, let's walk back to our lesson two by two.**

Circular Favorites

Say: **Let's play Circular Favorites. We'll walk in a circle while I ask a question. After I ask the question, you can call out your answers as we walk. Each time I ask a new question, we'll switch the direction our circle is going.**

Form a circle and hold hands. Have children practice walking clockwise in the circle (show them which direction to go), then have them practice changing direction to walk counter-clockwise. When everyone is ready, start the activity by asking one of the following questions while children walk around the circle in a clockwise motion:

● **What's your favorite food?** (Have children name foods they like. When everyone finishes, call "Change direction" and switch the direction of the circle.)

● **What's your favorite TV show?** (Have children name TV shows they like then change directions as above.)

● **What's your favorite song that we sing at church?** (Have children name songs then change direction.)

● **What's your favorite thing to look at in church?** (Have children name things they like to look at then change direction.)

● **What's your favorite thing about God?** (Have children name what they like about God then change direction.)

● **What's your favorite thing about our class time?** (Have children name what they like about class time.)

Then say: **Now let's sit down in our circle and get back to our lesson.**

Love Hops

Have children sit in a circle. Say: **Let's play Love Hops. We'll start with** (name a child sitting next to you) **and then take turns around the circle. When it's your turn, hop up and name something you love about church. Then hop back to your sitting position. Ready? Let's begin!**

After all children have had a turn, take your turn by hopping up and saying: **I love our lesson, so now let's all hop back to it.**

(*Variation:* Instead of having children name something they love about church, they could name something they love about moms (for Mother's Day), dads (for Father's Day), Christmas (during Advent), or another seasonal topic.)

SECTION 2

Wiggle Tamers

for
Grades K—3

Green and yellow Tag

(You'll need several sheets of both yellow and green construction paper.)

Before class, cut the construction paper into enough 2-inch-wide strips so that half the class will have yellow strips and the other half will have green. Then tape the two ends of each strip together to make headbands.

Have the children stand in a line. Distribute yellow headbands to every other child, then give green headbands to the rest. You will now have a yellow team and a green team. If necessary, join in this game so that both teams have the same number of players.

Say: **This game is called Green and Yellow Tag. When I say "green," everyone wearing a green headband is "It" and should try to tag as many people wearing yellow headbands as possible. When I say "yellow," everyone wearing yellow is It and should try to tag the kids wearing green.**

Tell kids it's OK if they get tagged more than once, but that they should do their best to avoid being tagged.

When everyone understands the rules, call out a color to begin the game. Play several rounds to allow kids to burn off energy, then stop the action and say: **Now let's race back to our lesson.**

28

Silly Snake

(You'll need a blindfold for each child.)

Have children form groups of four or five and ask all but one member of each group to put on blindfolds. Have the blindfolded children in each group stand in line behind the child who isn't blindfolded. Instruct them to hold onto the waists of the children in front of them.

Say: **We'll pretend that each group is a snake, and the person in the front of your line is the head of the snake. Wherever the head of the snake goes, the body follows.**

Tell children to follow your directions for "slithering" around the room. When the "snakes" are ready, give directions such as—

- Go slow
- Go fast
- Turn in a circle
- Move to a corner
- Wiggle
- Meet the other snakes in the middle of the room

Then say: **Now let's all hiss like snakes as we slither back to our lesson.**

Joseph's Coat

(You'll need two blindfolds.)

Ask a volunteer to play the part of Joseph. Have the rest of the children sit in a big circle. Let Joseph sit in the middle of the circle. Blindfold Joseph and lay the other blindfold behind him. Explain that the second blindfold is Joseph's "coat."

Say: **This is a game called Joseph's Coat. If I tap your shoulder, quietly tiptoe to pick up the coat, bring it back, and hide it behind your back. If Joseph hears you, he can say, "Who's taking my coat?" and you must return to your place in the circle. If you get the coat without Joseph hearing you, point to another person in the circle who will then call out, "Joseph, Joseph, who took your coat?"**

Then let Joseph remove the blindfold and guess who took his coat. Allow him three guesses. If Joseph guesses correctly, have him trade places with the child who took the coat. Repeat the activity several times, allowing a different person to be Joseph each time.

Wrap up the game by saying: **Now let's all tiptoe quietly back to our lesson.**

Salt and Pepper

Say: **Let's play Salt and Pepper. I'll whisper in your ear to tell you whether you are salt or pepper. Remember what I tell you and don't tell anyone else.**

Have children stand in a line. Whisper either "salt" or "pepper" in each child's ear. If necessary, join in the game so that both groups have an equal number of players.

Say: **Walk around the room. When I say "dinner-time!" call out what you are: either salt or pepper. Then find a partner from the other group so there's one salt and one pepper person in each pair of "shakers." Once you've found a partner, link arms and jump all around as if someone is shaking you onto a plate of food. When I say "salt and pepper!" re-form your line. Ready? Dinnertime!**

Play a few times, then say: **Let's shake ourselves back to our lesson.**

Many-Eyed Monster

(You'll need a crayon for each child and a large sheet of newsprint.)

Draw a large circle on the newsprint, leaving adequate room so children can draw both inside and outside the circle. Give each child a crayon and lay the newsprint in the middle of the floor.

Say: **We'll pretend that the circle on this paper can become a monster! Here's how: Everyone will skip around the room. Whenever I name a part of a monster, stop skipping and draw that part on the newsprint. Since you'll each be drawing the same thing on the paper, our monster will have a lot of the same parts! When you finish drawing, jump back up and start skipping around the paper again.**

Have the children start skipping around the paper. Every few seconds, name a part of the monster such as an eye, a mouth, a foot, an ear, a hand, hair, and a nose. Allow enough time for children to finish drawing each item before moving on to the next.

When the newsprint begins to fill up, say: **Let's hang the picture of our many-eyed monster near our lesson so he can see what will happen next.**

(*Note:* If you have more than 20 children in class, you may want to let the children create two separate monsters.)

Cotton Ball Collection

(You'll need cotton balls.)

Choose a volunteer to stand in the middle of the room with hands cupped together. Next, have the other children form a line. Give each person in line one cotton ball, then place the rest of the cotton balls on the floor at the end of the line.

Say: **Let's see how many cotton balls our volunteer can hold. When I say "go," take turns carefully placing a cotton ball in** (name)**'s hands. Then return to the end of the line and get another cotton ball. We'll keep stacking cotton balls until one finally falls. Remember, we need to do this very carefully because we need to balance as many cotton balls as we can in our volunteer's hands.**

When children are ready, say "go!" and let the activity begin. Keep a running count of how many cotton balls are balanced in the volunteer's hands. When a cotton ball falls, the game is over. Thank your volunteer and announce the total number of cotton balls balanced.

Then say: **You all did a great job! Give yourselves a round of applause before we get back to our lesson.**

Video Action

Choose one volunteer.

Say: **Everyone except our volunteer has just become a player on a video screen. Our volunteer will pretend to have a remote control. Instead of pressing buttons, he or she will call out the button he or she wants to push, such as fast forward, reverse, and play.**

If you hear the words, "fast forward," walk forward as fast as you can until you hear another word. If you hear the word "reverse," walk backward. If you hear the word "play," team up with two people, hold hands, and walk in a circle to the left.

During the activity choose different volunteers to call out video commands. Then gather the children together by saying: **Now let's "fast forward" to our lesson.**

Cruisin' Cars

Say: **We're going to play Cruisin' Cars. I'm going to name types of vehicles and I want you to move around the room just like those vehicles move. Make sounds like cars or trucks while you're moving. Ready? Start your engines!**

Name vehicles such as—

● A tractor
● A race car
● A fire truck
● A car running out of gas

Then say: **Choose any vehicle you want to be and we'll zoom back to our lesson.**

35

Shoe Tangle

Have children take off their shoes and put them in a pile.

Say: **We're going to play Shoe Tangle. When I say "go," find two shoes that don't match and try to put them on. It's OK if the shoes don't belong to you.**

After you have the two shoes on, walk around the room and find a match for one of the shoes that you're wearing. When you find a match, stand side by side with that person so your matching shoes touch. Then move with that person, keeping your matching shoes together. The activity is over when everyone in our class is connected by matching shoes.

Remind kids to be careful with other people's shoes, then say: **Let's find our own shoes so we can walk back to our lesson.**

36

What's Different?

Have children form pairs and stand face to face with their partners. Let partners decide who will be the Detective and who will be the Clue-giver during this activity.

Then have the Detectives turn away from their partners while the Clue-givers change one thing about their appearances. For example, a Clue-giver might unbutton a button, untie a shoe lace, roll up a pant leg, or put glasses on upside down. When Clue-givers are ready, have the Detectives turn around and see if they can guess what the Clue-givers have changed. Allow 30 to 60 seconds for Detectives to guess, then have Clue-givers reveal what they changed.

Have partners switch roles and repeat the activity. Then say: **Let's go see how our lesson can change our lives.**

Sneaky Shoe

(You'll need a coin and tape.)

Ask for three volunteers to come to the front of the room. Have the volunteers stand shoulder to shoulder, facing the class. Ask the rest of the children to turn and face the back of the room so they can't see the volunteers. Tape the coin to the bottom of one volunteer's shoe, then have all volunteers stand with their feet flat on the floor.

Allow the rest of the class to face the volunteers. Say: **There's a sneaky shoe among our volunteers, and it's hiding a coin! Let's see if we can guess which volunteer has the sneaky shoe. How many of you think our first volunteer's shoe is hiding the coin?** (Pause for children to respond.) **How many of you think our second volunteer's shoe is hiding the coin?** (Pause for children to respond.) **How many of you think our third volunteer's shoe is hiding the coin?** (Pause for children to respond.)

After everyone has voted, reveal where the coin is hidden. Then ask for three new volunteers and play again. Afterward, say: **Let's sneak our way back to our seats and see what's hidden in our lesson.**

Crocodile Snap

Let one child pretend to be a crocodile. Have that child hold both arms in front of him or her and snap them open and closed like a crocodile's mouth.

Say: **We're going to play Crocodile Snap. This crocodile will try to eat the rest of you, so you'll need to walk fast. If the crocodile snaps at you with its mouth and you get caught, then you become a hungry crocodile too! Soon we'll have nothing but crocodiles! Ready? Let's play!**

Allow children to play for several minutes. Then say: **Let's all make crocodile mouths and hurry back to our lesson.**

Partner Tag

(You'll need an outdoor area with plenty of open space for running.)

Take the children to an outdoor area and form pairs.

Say: **We're going to play Partner Tag. With your partner, decide who will be the Runner and who will be the Chaser. When I say "go," the Chaser will try to tag the Runner. If a Runner gets tagged, switch roles so the Runner becomes the Chaser. There will be lots of people running, so try not to bump into anyone else.**

When everyone understands the rules, start the activity. Let children play for a few minutes. Then say: **Let's chase each other back to our lesson.**

Hatching Eggs

(You'll need old newspaper.)

Have the children form a big circle, then let them each crumple up three or four sheets of newspaper and throw them into the middle of the circle.

Say: **I think it's time to play Hatching Eggs. We'll pretend that our newspaper balls are the eggs. When I say, "hatch eggs," squawk like a chicken and quickly gather three or four eggs. Once you have your eggs, sit on them like a mother hen would. Make sure no eggs are left without a parent to take care of them. If you see a lonely egg, jump up and add it to your nest.**

When kids are ready, let the fun begin. Play several rounds, then say: **Squawk like a chicken, grab three eggs, and sit on them back at our lesson.**

Season Switch

As a group, practice the following motions for the appropriate seasons:

- Spring—Pretend to plant seeds
- Summer—Pretend to swim
- Fall—Pretend to rake leaves
- Winter—Pretend to shovel snow

Say: **Now that we know all the motions, we can play Season Switch. We'll start by skipping around the room. When I call out a season, stop and do the motion for that season. When I say, "Season's over!" start skipping again. Ready? Start skipping!**

Play long enough for kids to "perform" each season at least once or twice. Then say: **Choose your favorite season and do that motion all the way back to our lesson.**

Mail and Deliver

(You'll need two to four buckets and an envelope for each child.)

Place the buckets at various places around the room and give an envelope to each child.

Say: **We're going to play Mail and Deliver. To begin, walk around the room. When I say "mail," run to the nearest bucket and drop your envelope in it. Then start walking around the room again. When I say "deliver," run to the nearest mailbox and grab one envelope.**

Repeat the activity several times.

Then say: **Let's pretend we're envelopes and mail ourselves back to our lesson.**

Footprint Frenzy

(You'll need a few shallow tubs of water.)

On a hot day, gather the children on a grassy area near a sidewalk. Set a few tubs of water nearby and let the children take off their shoes and socks.

Say: **This activity is called Footprint Frenzy. When I say "go," get your feet wet and then walk on the pavement as far as you can before you stop leaving footprints. Count the number of steps you take until you can no longer see any prints. Then we'll compare numbers.**

When the children have each had a turn, say: **That was fun! Now let's put our shoes back on and count how many steps it takes us to get back to our lesson.**

44

Tricky Toss

(You'll need a large, soft ball.)

Form a circle and say: **When I throw this ball in the air, run away from it as fast as you can—don't let the ball touch you as it falls to the ground. At the same time, I'll call out names of two people who can try to get the ball. Once someone gets the ball, he or she can yell "freeze" and everyone must stop. Then we'll see how far away from the ball everyone got before we had to freeze.**

When children understand the rules, start the game by gently lobbing the ball into the air and calling out two names. After everyone is "frozen," re-form the circle and play several more times. Then say: **Freeze! Let's toss the ball in the air and run back to our lesson.**

(*Variation:* For added fun, you may try bouncing the ball off a wall or the floor, or rolling the ball like a bowling ball.)

45

Jelly Bean Roll

(You'll need a bag of jelly beans.)

On one side of the room, have the children kneel side by side in a line. Place a jelly bean in front of each child.

Say: **When I say "go," roll your jelly bean across the room using only your nose. Remember, you can't touch the jelly bean with your hands. Ready? Go!**

Allow kids several minutes to roll their jelly beans. Then say: **Let's roll our jelly beans back to our lesson where I'll trade a clean, yummy jelly bean for your dirty one.**

Javelin Throw

(You'll need a plastic straw for each child.)

Use masking tape to place a 10- to 15-foot line on the floor. Have the children line up side by side behind the masking tape line with enough space between them so they'll have room to throw.

Give each child a straw and say: **We're going to play Javelin Throw. Your straw is the javelin. When I say "throw!" toss your straw as far in front of you as you can. Watch where it lands, then run to that place and stay there. When I say "throw!" again, toss your javelin back toward the tape line to see if you can get it across.**

Repeat the activity several times. Then say: **Now let's throw our javelins back to our lesson.**

(*Note:* During this activity, caution children not to throw straws at each other.)

Spoons, Forks, and Knives

Have children form three groups similar in size. Designate one group as the Spoons, another as the Forks, and the third as the Knives.

Say: **This game is called Spoons, Forks, and Knives. As you skip around the room I'll name a certain food. Decide whether you'd eat that food with a spoon, a fork, or a knife. If you're pretending to be that piece of silverware, come to the center of the room and share high fives with others like you. Then you'll all skip around the room again and I'll call out another type of food. Ready? Let's all start skipping!**

During the game, name foods such as—

- Soup
- Butter
- Salad
- Spaghetti
- Ice cream
- Cake

Then say: **Let's form a circle and go back to our lesson so we can "eat up" all there is to learn today.**

(*Note:* Eating soup with a knife would be difficult, but it's OK if children take some liberties during the game. For example, if children designated as knives circle up when you call out "soup," enjoy their creativity. Don't use this activity to teach kids about table etiquette—just let them have fun!)

Name Roll

(You'll need one ball of yarn and a watch with a second hand.)

Have children scatter around the room. Instruct each person to stand with feet about 12 inches apart.

Say: **We're going to play Name Roll. I'll start by tying one end of the yarn to my ankle. Next, I'll call out the name of one person in class and then roll the yarn ball between that person's feet. That person will then call out a new name and repeat the process. Let's see how long it'll take before we're all connected by the yarn.**

When all the children understand how to play, start the ball rolling. Use your timer to see how long it takes for everyone to become connected. Then, if you have time, collect the yarn and repeat the activity to see if you can finish faster the second time.

When you're ready to return to your lesson, say: **Now let's go get tangled up in the rest of our lesson!**

(*Variation:* For extra fun, you might have children call out names of Bible characters as they roll the yarn back and forth.)

48

Spin and Say

(You'll need a blindfold.)

Have everyone form a circle and choose one volunteer to stand in the center.

Say: **This game is called Spin and Say. Here's how to play. First we'll blindfold our volunteer. Then our volunteer will extend an arm straight ahead and slowly turn as if he or she were the spinner on a game board. While the volunteer is spinning, the rest of us will count to five. When we reach the number five, the volunteer will stop turning but will keep the blindfold on.**

Whoever the volunteer is pointing to can give us all one simple command such as "bark like a dog," "hug the teacher," or "hop up and down." Then I'll choose a new volunteer and start again.

Make sure that children understand the rules, then start the game. Do your best to pace the counting so that a different child is picked each time.

When you're ready to finish, say: **Now let's all close our eyes and slowly spin around one time before we get back to our lesson.**

Sidewalk Snake

(You'll need colored chalk.)

As weather permits, take the children outside to a sidewalk or a safe area of open pavement. Let the children draw a huge snake from one end of the pavement to the other. Encourage them to make a creative head and tail for their snake. Ask for one or two volunteers to draw the snake's outline while the other children decorate the body.

Once children finish, have them line up single file at the head.

Say: **We're going to play Sidewalk Snake. When I say "gulp!" the first person in line will pretend to be swallowed by our snake by running along the entire snake all the way to its tail. As soon as that person gets to the tail he or she must wait there while the next person gets swallowed. We'll see how full we can make the snake.**

When the last child has had a turn, say: **Let's escape from the snake's mouth and run back to our lesson.**

(*Note:* If you're short on time, have kids draw only the head and tail of the snake while you draw the middle area.)

under Construction

Have everyone choose an unbreakable item in the room and bring it back to a circle.

Say: **Starting with** (name)**, let's take turns stacking our items to build a tower.**

Have the children build a tower by balancing one object on top of another. If the tower falls, allow children to rearrange the parts of the tower and to restack their objects. Continue as long as time allows or until the tower is finished.

Then say: **Let's take apart our tower so we can go back to our lesson.**

(*Variation:* If you'd like, you could use Duplo or large Lego blocks and have kids build a tower using blocks of—

- The same color
- Different colors
- The same size
- Different sizes)

Wiggle Tamers

for
Grades 4—6

String Along

(You'll need yarn and scissors.)

Have each child cut five to seven pieces of yarn of various lengths. Then have the children place their yarn on the floor throughout the room.

Say: **Let's spread out across the room to play String Along. The goal of this game is for everyone to be linked together with this yarn—but we'll have to do it within a two-minute time limit.**

Have kids spread out across the room and sit down. Tell kids they must remain in their places during the entire game.

Say: **When I say "go," grab as many pieces of yarn as you can from where you're sitting. Tie those pieces together to form a long string. Hang on to one end of your string and toss the other end to someone nearby. After two minutes I'll say "stop," and we'll see how well we did. Ready? Go!**

End the game after a couple of minutes and say: **Let's form one long string by tying the ends of our yarn together. Then hang on and we'll "string" our way back to our lesson.**

53

Square Scramble

Form groups of four or five.

Say: **Form the four corners of a square with the people in your group. If you have five people in your group, have the fifth person stand in the middle of your square.**

Memorize exactly where everyone is standing so that after we scramble you'll be able to make the same square again.

Then say: **When I say "scramble," leave your squares and speed-walk around the room. When I say "square off," find your original group and create your same square in a different part of the room. When you've created the square, call "squared!"**

Repeat the activity three or four times, then say: **Let's scramble back to our lesson.**

54

Noisy Car

Form groups of four or five.

Say: **In each group, everyone must choose a different noisy part of a car, such as a muffler, a horn, an engine, a flat tire, or a turn signal. Then you'll link arms with the other members of your group and "drive" around the room while making your noises. When I say "green light," start driving. When I say "red light," stop and make a quiet engine sound until I say "green light" again.**

Alternate the commands a few times, then say: **Now let's drive back to our lesson!**

It Flies!

Have a volunteer carefully stand on a chair in front of the class.

Say: **Let's play It Flies! Our volunteer will name things that fly while everyone else runs around the room imitating that flying thing. Listen closely, though, because when the person on the chair names something that *doesn't* fly, you must stop immediately and place your arms at your sides. If the person on the chair sees you moving and calls out your name, you're out of the game and must sit down until the next round.**

Begin the activity. If the volunteer has trouble thinking of things to name, suggest the following: birds, pigeons, airplanes, ducks, kangaroos, cars, bees, and turtles. Help as needed in determining who should be out of the game. Then let a new person be the caller and play again.

After a few rounds of this game, say: **That's enough flying for one day. Now let's land back at our lesson.**

Beat the Clock

Form groups of six or seven. Have each group sit in its own circle. Choose one person from each group to be the Tapper.

Say: **For this game, I'll call out a letter of the alphabet. The Tapper in each group will jump up and walk around the circle tapping each person while naming an item that starts with that letter. Each item must be different. For example, if I call out H, the Tapper can use words such as "hippo," "hammer," "horse," "hamburger," and so on. See how many people you can tap in 15 seconds. Each time I call out a new letter, let someone else be the Tapper.**

When kids understand the rules, start the activity. Every 15 seconds call out a new letter. Play until everyone has had at least one turn to be the Tapper.

Then say: **Well, our game is over so it's time to tap back into our lesson.**

Animal Roar

Form a circle. Have the person on your right say a short sentence that includes an animal name, an animal sound, and a movement. For example, the child might say, "Tigers growl and jump." Have everyone in the group make that animal sound and perform the action.

Then have the next person change one word of the original sentence. For example, this person might say, "Tigers squeak and jump." Have the group make this new noise and perform the action. For extra fun, let each child try to repeat all the animal sounds and actions that have become part of the sentence. Then let the group make all the noises and perform all the actions.

Continue in this manner until everyone has had a turn to change the sentence. Then say: **Children play then hurry back to the lesson. Let's go!**

Bubble Tag

Form groups of three or four. Have the members of each group hold hands in a circle.

Choose one group to be "It." Say: **We'll pretend that each group is a bubble. The goal is to remain in your bubble without being tagged by the bubble that is It. If you're tagged, your bubble bursts and all members of your group must join the "It bubble." That means the It bubble will get bigger each time someone in another bubble is tagged.**

Play the game twice, then have the original bubble group chase everyone back to the lesson.

Button Battle

(You'll need masking tape, paper clips, and a bunch of buttons.)

Have children line up next to each other on one side of the room. Use masking tape to mark a finish line across the floor on the opposite side of the room. Give each child a button and a paper clip.

Say: **We're going to play Button Battle. When I say "go," use your paper clip to nudge or flip your button to the finish line. Remember—no hands allowed on the button itself. May the best button win!**

For extra fun, have children name their buttons and cheer them on by name. When all the buttons have been moved across the finish line, say: **What a race! Hand your buttons to me as we go back to our lesson.**

Shoe Shuffle

(You'll need yarn and a pair of scissors.)

Form groups of six and have members of each group stand side by side in a line.

Say: **We're going to play Shoe Shuffle. Untie your shoelaces, then tie one of your laces to the lace of the person on your right. Tie the other lace to the lace of the person on your left. If you don't have shoelaces, use pieces of yarn to wrap around your shoes and tie to your neighbors' laces.**

After children have tied their laces together, say: **Now try to walk six feet forward without falling down. Go slowly.**

Then say: **OK, now we can untie ourselves and shuffle back to our lesson.**

Roll the Box

(You'll need two large, square cardboard boxes taped shut; and a thick marker.)

Before this activity, prepare two boxes in the following manner: On box #1, write one of these words on each side:

- Running
- Jumping
- Dancing
- Rolling
- Skipping
- Singing

On box #2, write one of these instructions on each side:

- Alone
- With a partner
- In groups of three
- In groups of four
- In groups of five
- Whole group

Say: **We're going to play Roll the Box. When I call out the names of two class members, they must each run, pick up a box, and toss it away from the rest of the group. Then everyone will do the actions written on the tops of the boxes.**

Repeat the activity until you've called the name of each group member at least once. Then say: **Let's roll the boxes one last time. We'll follow the directions to get back to our lesson.**

Newspaper Shuffle

(You'll need a stack of newspapers.)

Form two teams and give each team member two sections of a newspaper. Then have both teams line up at one end of the room.

Say: **The goal of this game is to race to the opposite side of the room without stepping on the floor. Put one section of the newspaper in front of you and stand on it. Then put the next section of newspaper in front of that one and stand on it. Pick up the newspaper behind you (without touching the floor) so that you can use that section to move forward again. When one team member reaches the wall at the other side of the room, the next player on the team may start across.**

Continue play until everyone has had a turn to cross the room.

Then say: **Now let's do the "newspaper shuffle" all the way back to the late-breaking news of our lesson.**

The Neighbor's Pet

Have the children form a circle.

Say: **Let's play The Neighbor's Pet. One person will think of a pet—for example, a dog—and say, "The neighbor's dog never sits still. It always does this." When you say "this," add a noise or motion to match the pet, such as barking like a dog. Then everyone must repeat that motion.**

Then have the next person in the circle think of a different pet and repeat the process. Continue around the circle until each person has named a pet.

When it's your turn, say: **The neighbor's pet never sits still. It always does this...** and lead kids back to the lesson.

Loony Legs

(You'll need masking tape.)

Form two teams of equal number. Ask an adult to join a team if needed. Have the teams line up single file at one end of the room. Using masking tape, place a finish line on the floor about 20 feet away.

Say: **When I call out a number between zero and two, the first person in each line will race to the finish line. If I say "two," that person may run. If I say "one," he or she must hop on one foot. If I say "zero," two team-mates must carry that person to the finish line, then run back to the start for their turns. We'll continue until both teams finish the race.**

Start the game, calling out different numbers for each set of runners.

Then say: **Let's make it easy and use two legs to walk back to our lesson.**

Scrabble Scramble

(You'll need construction paper and markers.)

Have children write the letters of the alphabet on sheets of construction paper—one letter per sheet. Include two sheets each for the letters A, H, N, S, and T, and three sheets each for the letters E and O.

Next, distribute the papers as evenly as possible among the children in class until all the letters are distributed. If there are more students than papers, have children share letters.

When everyone is ready, play Scrabble Scramble. As you name Bible characters, have the children hold their letters up and arrange themselves to spell that name.

Use familiar names such as—

- God
- Jesus
- Queen Esther
- Adam
- King Solomon
- Zechariah
- Bartholomew
- Paul
- Queen Vashti
- Felix
- Mary

Wrap up by saying: **Let's spell the word "lesson" before scrambling back to it.**

Snow Tag

On a wintry day, take the children out to a play area freshly covered with snow. Have kids outline a 20-foot circle by stomping in the snow. Choose one or two volunteers to be "It."

Say: **This game is a snowy version of Tag. Here's how to play: We'll all start out inside the circle. When I say "go," It can begin chasing and tagging other players. To get away from It, you can leave the circle and create new paths in the snow. However, It cannot create a new path in the snow. In order for It to leave the circle, he or she must only run in paths where others have run. Anyone tagged becomes Its partner and joins in chasing the other players.**

When everyone understands the rules, shout "go!" to begin the game. Allow kids to play until everyone has been tagged or until time is up. To speed up the game, designate several people to be It.

When you're ready to head back indoors, say: **Let's all make new tracks back to our lesson.**

(*Variation:* During the summer season you may want to use tubs of water and have kids make trails of watery footprints instead of snowy paths.)

67

Back to Back

(You'll need two balloons for each team and a playing field.)

Form teams of six players each. You can also have a few teams of four players, but you must have an even number of children on each team. Ask adults to join a team if you need a few more players.

Have each child find a partner on his or her team. Ask pairs on each team to space themselves equally from one end of the playing field to the other—about 20 feet apart.

Have partners stand back to back, linking their arms behind them. Give the first pair on each team two inflated balloons: one for each child to carry.

When I say "go," the first pair on each team will walk toward the next pair—one child walks forward while the other child walks backward. Both must hold on to their balloons. If one drops a balloon, they cannot unlink their arms but must work together to pick up the fallen balloon.

When the first pair reaches the next pair, the children will hand their balloons to that pair who will then proceed to the last pair. The race is over when the balloons have been moved from one end of the field to the other.

If a team has only four players, have the first two players take the position of the third pair once they hand their balloons to the second pair.

Then say: **With your partner, stand back to back, link arms, and head back to our lesson.**

Finding Feelings

(You'll need paper and pencils.)

Have children form groups of three or four with people who have sock colors that match theirs. If necessary, form a group of mixed colors. Give each group a sheet of paper and a pencil. Read the following list aloud while one person in each group writes it down:

- Nervous
- Happy
- Proud
- Scared
- Sad
- Confused
- Angry
- Excited
- Cheerful
- Loved
- Funny

Then say: **I think it's time for a Feelings Scavenger-Hunt.**

Take all the groups outdoors, then say: **For each feeling listed on your paper, find an object that represents that feeling. For example, a piece of litter might represent a sad feeling because you feel sad when you see pollution. Or a dandelion might represent a happy feeling because dandelions remind you of summertime. You'll have three minutes to find as many items as you can with your group. Ready? Go.**

After a few minutes, call everyone together and allow groups to share about the items they gathered. Then say: **You did a good job finding things that represent feelings. Now let's go inside and see if we can find the rest of our lesson!**

69

Pass the Ball

(You'll need one ball.)

Have children stand in a circle and give one child the ball.

Say: **The person with the ball will come up with a fancy or fun way to pass the ball to the person on his or her right. Then that person will pass the ball in the same way to the right, and so on, until the ball has been passed all the way around. When the ball has traveled around the circle once, a different person will choose a new way to pass the ball. We'll continue until everyone has chosen a fun and creative way to pass the ball.**

When everyone has had a turn, say: **Let's pass the ball back and forth as we head back to our lesson.**

70

Travel Twister

Form a circle and ask a volunteer to stand in the middle.

Say: **Our volunteer will be the leader for this game. Our leader will name a place such as a city or state, an animal that starts with the same letter as that place, and a way to move that starts with the same letter.**

For example, our leader might say, "I'm going to Boston as a bear and I'm bouncing there." Then the rest of us must move around in a circle, making that animal noise and performing that action.

Give the volunteer a moment to think of what he or she will say, then begin the activity.

Allow several children to have a turn acting as the leader before you wrap up by saying: **Let's go back to the lesson as lions and we'll *leap* there.**

Squirt Away!

(You'll need a squirt bottle for each child. Use empty shampoo or food bottles with squirt tops. You'll also need water and a piece of chalk.)

Do this activity outdoors on a nice, warm day. Use the chalk to draw two parallel lines about 12 feet apart on a sidewalk or parking lot. Give each child a squirt bottle to fill with water. Then have kids stand next to each other behind one of the lines.

Say: **We're going to play Squirt Away! When I say "go," squeeze your bottles to see who can squirt water the farthest toward the other line.**

When children have emptied their bottles, let them "reload" and try to wash away both chalk lines.

Then say: **Let's put these bottles away before we get back to our lesson.**

12

Stepping Stones

(You'll need 12 empty coffee cans.)

This activity works best outdoors on a level, grassy field. If you do this activity indoors, choose an area with a soft carpeted floor so the coffee cans don't slip.

Form two teams of equal number. Ask an adult to join a team if necessary. Have the teams line up single file on one side of the room, facing the same direction. In front of each team, place six empty coffee cans—upside down—in a straight line extending toward the other side of the room. Space the cans about one foot apart from each other, like stepping stones.

Say: **When I say "go," the first person on each team must step onto the first coffee can and carefully walk across the six cans to get to the other side. Then the second person will walk across the cans. Continue until everyone on a team has made it to the other side. If you fall off a can, you may go to the end of your team's line and try again when your turn comes up or skip the rest of your turn.**

When everyone finishes, say: **Let's imagine we're walking on stepping stones as we head back to our lesson.**

(*Note:* For safety's sake, you may want to station volunteers on either side of the two teams to help kids in case they fall off the cans.)

Construction Paper Tag

(You'll need red and blue construction paper. Half the class will use red, and the other half will use blue. If desired, you may use any two colors you choose.)

Form two teams—team A and team B. Give each member of team A one sheet of red construction paper, and each member of team B one sheet of blue construction paper. Have the children spread out in the room.

Say: **When I say "go," balance your construction paper on your head and start walking around the room. People with the red paper must then try to tag those with the blue paper. If you're tagged, you must sit out of the game. If the paper falls off your head, quickly pick it up and put it back on. If you're tagged by someone whose paper has fallen off, you're still in the game.**

Start the game. When the last child is tagged, have kids switch colors and repeat the game.

Then say: **Let's see if we can balance the paper on our heads all the way back to our lesson.**

Tightrope Totter

(You'll need two pieces of chalk or two rolls of masking tape.)

Form two teams. Have each team make a "tightrope" by marking on the ground with chalk if you're outdoors or masking tape if you're indoors. Encourage teams to be creative and make zigzags and curlicues for their tightropes. Warn them, however, that the markings must be continuous and easy to walk on.

When the tightropes are completed, have team members line up single file at one end of the opposing team's tightrope. Then let them begin walking on the tightrope, being careful not to fall off. After the first child of each team has taken five steps, have the next child begin to walk the tightrope.

When everyone is finished, say: **Now let's walk an imaginary tightrope back to our lesson.**

Balloon Burst

(This is a fun activity for a sunny day. You'll need a balloon for each child, water, chalk, and three magnifying glasses.)

Form three teams equal in number. Any extra children can be judges. Help each child fill a balloon with water and tie it.

With chalk, draw a starting line on the ground. Then draw another line parallel to that one about 20 feet away. Have teams set their balloons on this line then stand single file behind the starting line.

Say: **We're going to play Balloon Burst. The first person on each team will receive a magnifying glass. When I say "go," those players must run to a balloon and hold the magnifying glass near it so the sun creates heat on its surface. Within a few seconds, the intense heat should pop the balloon. When a team member's balloon pops, that player will run back to the starting line and hand the magnifying glass to the next person on his or her team.**

Continue until everyone has completed the race.

If someone has difficulty getting a balloon to pop, allow that person to break the balloon by stomping on it.

Then say: **Let's use our magnifying glasses to find our way back to the lesson.**

Alphabet Leap

Form two teams of equal number.

Have teams sit in two circles with one team forming an outside circle and the other team forming an inside circle. Have the two teams face each other, sitting so their feet are touching the feet of the person opposite them. Space pairs about two feet apart if possible.

Say: **We're going to play Alphabet Leap. When I call out a letter of the alphabet, jump up if your first or last name starts with that letter. For example, if I say "L," Lisa, Linda, Lonnie, and Jack Larson would all jump up. Then they would hop around the circle to the right until they got back to their original places.**

Repeat the activity using each letter of the alphabet. Then say: **Now that we've used up that extra energy, we can get back to our lesson.**

SECTION 4

Wiggle Tamers

for Mixed Ages

Name Jumble

Ask a volunteer to stand next to you and be "It." Have the rest of the children sit in a circle.

Say: **This game is like Duck, Duck, Goose; but with a twist. The person who is It will walk around the circle and pat each person on the head while saying that person's first name. When It says an incorrect name—either on purpose or not—that person must jump up and chase It around the circle. If It runs around the circle and sits in the chaser's place without being tagged, the chaser becomes It and starts the game again. If It is tagged, he or she must sit in the middle of the circle until someone else is caught and takes his or her place.**

Have the children play the game a number of times.

Then say: **Let's all shout our first names at the same time and chase each other back to our lesson.**

Scarf Snag

(You'll need one scarf or bandanna for each child.)

Choose three volunteers, then distribute a scarf to each child except those three. Instruct the children to either put their scarves in their back pockets or stuff them into their shirt sleeves. Make sure they each leave at least a 3-inch tail sticking out.

Say: **We're going to play Scarf Snag. The three players who don't have scarves will chase the rest of you to snag yours. If someone gets your scarf, then you and that person must switch roles.**

When everyone understands the rules, begin the game by saying: **Ready? Snag!**

After the game, say: **Rearrange your scarves and I'll chase you back to our lesson.**

Doctor, Help!

(You'll need a box of facial tissues.)

Choose a volunteer to be the doctor then give that person a full box of facial tissues.

Say: **This game is called Doctor, Help! When I say "go," run around the room. Whenever you feel like it, pretend to sneeze. The doctor will then run after you to give you a tissue. Once you have a tissue, keep sneezing. The doctor will only give you one tissue, but you may keep sneezing even when you have a tissue.**

Play until everyone has at least one facial tissue.

Then say: **Let's all sneeze our way back to the lesson.**

(*Note:* For younger children, simplify this activity by having the doctor give children a tissue every time they sneeze.)

Foot Tag

(You'll need at least one squirt bottle filled with water.)

On a warm day, allow the children to take off their socks and shoes, then take the class outdoors. Choose a volunteer to be "It," and give that person a squirt bottle full of water.

Say: **We're going to play Foot Tag. Here are the rules: When I say "go," everyone will run away from It. The only way It can tag you is by squirting your feet. Once your feet get wet, you must sit down for the rest of the round. We'll play for one minute, then give someone else a chance to be It. Ready? Go!**

Play as many rounds as you like. Afterward, form a circle and squirt everyone's feet.

Say: **Now that everybody's been tagged, let's "squirt" our way back to our lesson.**

(*Variation:* If you have more than a dozen children in class, you may consider having two "Its.")

Painter, Painter

(You'll need a chair for each child except one.)

Arrange the chairs in a circle. Select a volunteer to be the painter, and have everyone else secretly choose to "be" one of the following colors: red, green, gold, silver, or yellow.

Say: **For this game, the painter will name a color. Anyone who has chosen that color must jump up and switch chairs with another person who has the same color. However, once you jump up, the painter may quickly sit on any empty chair. The person left without a chair will be the new painter. The painter can either name one color at a time or say "rainbow." If the painter says "rainbow," everyone must jump up and switch chairs.**

Play the game five or six times, then say: **When I call out a color, anyone who chose that color must hurry back to our lesson. Ready? Rainbow!**

Ball Hop

(You'll need 10 to 15 cotton balls.)

Create a cotton-ball trail using 10 to 15 cotton balls. Place them at least two feet apart. Have children stand in a single-file line behind the first cotton ball in the trail.

Say: **On the word "go," the first person in line will run up to the first cotton ball and hop over it, then run to the second cotton ball and hop over it and so on until he or she has hopped over all the cotton balls. Then that person will run to the back of the line. Once the first person has hopped over two balls, the next person in line can start.**

Have children run the course twice. Then have kids help you rearrange the balls so they lead back to your lesson area.

Say: **Let's follow the trail back to our lesson.**

Bounce the Balls!

(You'll need one bouncing ball for each child. Use a variety of balls—tennis balls, soccer balls, Ping-Pong balls, etc.)

Have the kids spread out across the room and sit down. Give each person a ball. If there aren't enough for each child to have one, have kids share in pairs or trios.

Then say: **The object of this game is to get a new ball without moving from your seat. Here's what we'll do: When I say "bounce!" that'll be your cue to gently bounce your ball across the floor. We'll all bounce our balls at the same time.**

Keep the balls bouncing until I say, "Stop that bouncing!" Then do your best to grab a ball near you without moving from your seat.

When kids are ready, start the game by calling out "bounce!"

Play three or four rounds, then say: **Let's each find a ball and bounce it back to our lesson.**

Peanut Butter

Say: **It's time for the Peanut Butter Game!**

When I say "go," hop around the room. Whenever I say, "peanut butter," stick to the people closest to you, no matter how many there are.

Then, when I say "jelly," unstick yourselves and hop around the room again. Ready? Go!

Play four or five rounds. Then say: **Let's sit down now so we can stick to our lesson.**

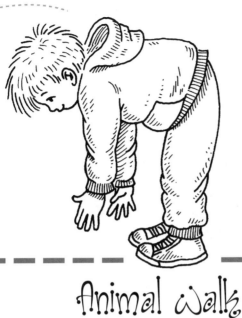

Animal Walk

Say: **Let's play Animal Walk.** Have the kids stand in a line with a volunteer at the head of the line.

Then say: **I'm going to name an animal. Our volunteer will imitate that animal by moving around the room and making sounds that animal would make. After our volunteer shows us what to do, the rest of us will follow him or her around the room imitating the sounds and gestures.**

Every so often, I'll stop the "animal walk" and ask for a new volunteer to lead us in imitating a new animal. Ready? Let's start with a lion!

Play as many rounds as you like. Name animals such as—

- A crocodile
- An elephant
- A dinosaur
- A parrot
- A monkey

Afterward, say: **Now let's imitate mice and scurry back to our lesson.**

Squirt Tag

(You'll need one squirt bottle filled with water.)

Use this activity in a setting where kids can get wet, such as on a retreat or during a summer day-program.

On a warm day, take the children outside to a grassy play area. Choose a volunteer to be the Squirter. Give the Squirter a squirt bottle filled with water.

Say: **We're going to play Squirt Tag. The Squirter will try to get others wet by squirting water at them. When I say "squirt!" run around and see how long you can stay dry.**

Remind the Squirter not to aim at people's faces, then begin the game. When everyone is wet, give a new volunteer the squirt bottle to use to chase the Squirter with.

Then say: **Now that we're all wet, let's splash back to our lesson.**

People Ahoy

Have children skip around the room. Whenever you say, "I spy someone," have children stop and cup their hands around their eyes as if looking through a telescope. Then have them reply, "People ahoy! I see (name of a person they see through their imaginary telescopes)."

When you call, "Set sail!" have children run around again.

Then cup your hands around your eyes and say: **Lesson ahoy! The lesson is waiting for us! I see it! Let's go!**

Motion Commotion

Say: **Let's play an acting game called Motion Commotion. Every time I describe a motion, perform that action twice. When I use the word "I," stand alone to do the motion. When I use the word "we," face the person closest to you to do the motion.**

Play along as you call out the following actions:

- **I can squirm.**
- **We can squirm.**
- **I can jump.**
- **We can jump.**
- **I can fall.**
- **We can fall.**
- **I can hop.**
- **We can hop.**
- **I can stretch.**
- **We can stretch.**
- **I can hug.**
- **We can hug.**

Then say: **Now we can walk back to the lesson.**

Colorful Fences

(You'll need yarn balls of various colors.)

As weather permits, take the children outside. Let them weave lengths of yarn in a fence near the church. Older children might create a design that zigzags, intersects, and curves. Younger children may want to include sticks and large leaves in the design.

If your church doesn't have a fence, let kids decorate a tree or bush. Children can wrap yarn around the trunk and weave it through the branches.

Then say: **Now let's pretend we're the yarn as we zigzag and weave back to our lesson.**

(*Note:* Remind kids to remove their artwork before they leave the church.)

Snow and Seek

(You'll need 10 nonpaper objects such as a coffee can, a plastic bottle, a pencil, and so on.)

On a snowy day, arrive at church early and bury the 10 objects in the snow. Make lots of footprints in the snow, to camouflage the footprints near the hiding spots.

If you live in a warm climate, consider hiding the objects in a sandbox or around the landscape.

Take the children outside and tell them to find the 10 treasures you've hidden in the snow. As they uncover the objects, ask the kids to bring the items to you.

Once every object has been found, say: **Now that you've found all these treasures, let's see what treasures we can find in our lesson.**

Scoop!

(You'll need several balls of assorted sizes—the more the better.)

If possible, play this game outdoors or in a large room. Scatter all the balls around the room or play area.

Say: **It's time to play Scoop! Here's what to do: Walk around the room without stepping on any of the balls. When I say "scoop!" grab as many balls as you can and run with them. If you drop one, someone else can pick it up. When I say "unscoop!" drop the balls onto the floor. Ready? Scoop!**

As the children play, caution them to be careful so they don't bump heads, run into each other, or slip on a ball. Play the game four or five times, then call kids back together.

Say: **Let's scoop up all the balls and take them back to our lesson.**

Jell-O Jiggle

Choose a volunteer to lead the group for this activity, or lead the group yourself if your group has younger children.

Say: **Let's pretend that our class is a huge bowl of Jell-O. When one part of the Jell-O starts to jiggle, the entire bowl will begin jiggling in the same way. Our leader will start by doing a jiggling Jell-O imitation, then everyone else will follow by doing the same body motion. The leader can change the motion after he or she sees everyone doing the same motion.**

Have the volunteer lead the rest of the group in two or three different Jell-O motions. Then say: **Let's jiggle back to our lesson.**

Back to Basics

(You'll need a sheet of paper and a marker.)

Using a marker, draw a single picture on a sheet of paper but don't let the kids see what you've drawn. Choose a shape that your children will easily recognize, such as a heart, a house, a teddy bear, or a tree.

Ask children to stand quietly in a single-file line facing the same direction. Tell kids that in order to make this activity fun, they can't talk at all.

Show the picture that you've drawn to the child at the end of the line. Then have that child use his or her finger as a pencil to "draw" the picture on the back of the next child, who will draw it on the back of the *next* child, and so on. Continue the process until the picture reaches the front of the line. Then have the first child in line tell what picture he or she thinks was drawn.

Show the original drawing to the kids and let them giggle about their artistic interpretations.

Then say: **Now let's return to our lesson so we can "draw" the most learning out of it.**

That's Me!

Have children spread out in a large area and ask them to sit.

Say: **When I name something that describes you, jump up and shout, "That's me!" and then sit down again. Pay close attention when people jump up so you can learn more about them.**

Name descriptions such as—

- Likes to color
- Has a pet
- Lives in an apartment
- Likes to eat at McDonald's
- Has a brother
- Likes to ride a bike
- Likes winter best

End with "is in this class." Then say: **Since we're all in this class, let's jump up and get back to our lesson.**

Cotton Ball Catastrophe

(You'll need a bag of cotton balls and a bucket.)

This activity requires a large open play area such as a field or recreation room. Place a bucket at one end of the area and take the bag of cotton balls to the other end. Open the bag and scatter the cotton balls all around.

Say: **Oh no! I've created a cotton ball catastrophe. We'll need to pick up all the cotton balls and place them in that bucket over there. But there's one rule we must follow: We can carry only one cotton ball at a time. Let's go!**

Once all the cotton balls are in the bucket, pick up the bucket and head back to the class. On the way, drop a bunch of the cotton balls again.

Then say: **Oh, dear! I've created another cotton ball catastrophe. This time, pick up the cotton balls as fast as you can so we can hurry back to our lesson.**

Color Tag

Say: **This seems like a good time to play Color Tag. Look at the colors you're wearing (not counting your shoes and socks). I'll name a color. If you *aren't* wearing that color, try to tag someone who is. If you *are* wearing that color, run and try not to be tagged.**

Once you're tagged, freeze in that position until we start the game again.

When kids understand the rules, start the game by calling out "blue!" Play as many rounds as you like. Finish the game by saying: **If you're wearing blue, chase everyone else back to the lesson.**

Cups of Water

(You'll need a paper cup for each child, four buckets, and water.)

On a warm day, take the children outside and form two teams equal in number. If necessary, ask an adult to join a team.

Have each team form a line parallel to the other team. Place a full bucket of water at one end of each line and an empty bucket at the other end. Give each child a paper cup.

Say: **We're going to play Cups of Water. When I say "go," the person standing next to the bucket of water must fill his or her cup and then pour the water into the second person's cup. That person will pour the water into the third person's cup, and so on. As soon as the first person has emptied a cup, he or she can fill another cup of water from the bucket. The goal is to fill the empty bucket at the end of each line with water. The first team to move all the water from one bucket to the other wins.**

Say: **Now let's take our cups and buckets back to the classroom and get back to our lesson.**

In the Ark?

(You'll need newsprint and markers.)

This idea is fun when your class is learning about the story of Noah and the ark.

Form groups of no more than four. (It's OK to have a few groups of three or five depending on how many children you have.) Give each group a sheet of newsprint and a marker. Have each group designate one person to be the recorder who writes all the group's ideas on the newsprint.

Say: **As a group, brainstorm the names of as many different animals as you can think of. Every time you list five animals, jump up and clap your hands five times. Then continue adding more animal names until I call time. When time is up, we'll see how many animals each group has named.**

Allow the kids to do the activity for three to five minutes, then call time. Have groups count how many animals they named. If time permits, have groups name all of their animals.

Say: **Let's give each other a big round of applause before we go back to our lesson.**

Toilet Paper Roll

(You'll need masking tape and four rolls of toilet paper.)

You'll need a large playing area for this activity. Form three groups and give each group a roll of toilet paper. With masking tape, mark a starting line at one end of the room and a finish line at the other.

Say: **We're going to play Toilet Paper Roll. The goal is to roll the toilet paper from the starting line to the finish line without letting it tear. Work together to make your toilet paper roll as straight as possible. If your toilet paper tears, have someone hold the end of the paper and continue rolling toward the finish line.**

After the activity have the children gather the toilet paper. Then say: **Now let's roll back to our lesson.**

Old Groups

Have the children jump around the room like frogs.

Say: **Whenever I call out how old I am, form groups of the number I mentioned. For example, if I say, "I'm four years old," form groups of four.**

After you've called out an age and children have formed groups, tell them to jump around the room like frogs again until you call out a different age.

Then say: **Now let's jump back to the lesson.**

Nature Catch

Use this activity on a day when leaves or snowflakes are falling outside.

Say: **I wonder if a person could catch leaves or snowflakes as they fell from the sky. Let's pretend we're catching those things right now!**

Let the children show you how they'd catch leaves in their hands or snow on their tongues. Then say: **You all look as though you could really do it! Let's go outside and try it on the real thing.**

Take the children outside and let them try to catch leaves in their hands or snow on their tongues.

After a few minutes, say: **Now that we've caught things outside, let's go inside and see what we can catch from our lesson.**